The Art of Batik
Flowers and Landscapes

For Forbes, Timothy and George.

The Art of Batik
Flowers and Landscapes

Mary Taylor

SEARCH PRESS

First published in Great Britain 1995

Search Press Limited
Wellwood, North Farm Road,
Tunbridge Wells, Kent, TN2 3DR

Photographs by Forbes Taylor, with the exception of those on pages 10 (right), 12, 13 (top), 14/15, 16 and 24 which are by Search Press Studio.

ISBN 0 85532 785 5

If you have any difficulty in getting any of the materials in this book, please write to the Publishers for a list of suppliers.

Search Press Limited
Wellwood, North Farm Road,
Tunbridge Wells, Kent TN2 3DR

The author would like to mention that several of the pictures illustrated in this book are in private collections. The pictures on pages 5 and 43 belong to Mr and Mrs L. Keen, that on page 6 belongs to Mrs S. Calver, that on page 7 to Mrs M. Evans, that on page 23 is in the Edith Cavell Hospital, Peterborough, that on page 36 belongs to Mr and Mrs W. J. Irving, that on page 39 to Mrs V. Thorne, that on page 40 to Mrs A. Eades, that on page 41 to Mr and Mrs M. Edwards, that on page 44 to Mr and Mrs C. Ingram, that on page 64 to Mr and Mrs G. Dannell, that on page 69 to Mrs L. Taylor, those on pages 72 and 73 to Mr and Mrs A. Percival, that on page 77 to Major-General and Mrs J. Stanyer, that on page 78 to Mr and Mrs R. H. Myddleton and that on page 80 to Mrs Frances Punnett.

The Publishers would like to thank Candlemakers Supplies for the selection of waxes shown in the photograph on page 12.

Printed in Spain by Elkar S. Coop., Bilbao 48012.

The author is indebted to Stanley Crossland and the late Michael O'Connell who both introduced her to the art of batik.

Front cover: **Dahlias.** A batik designed specifically for the cover of this book – see also the detail on page 23.

Page 1: The author brushing wax on to a landscape batik, using her original colour sketch as a reference.

*Page 3: **Meconopsis.** I wanted a light background to help keep a delicate quality in the pale blue petals. Many blue dyes went on, slowly deepening to produce the intended result.*

*Page 5: **Windy day, Walberswick.** This is a large 120 x 90cm (48 x 36in) picture that has a limited colour range. The light sky had to be waxed first, and kept waxed throughout. The bushes were carefully drawn in and the background was waxed 'behind' them.*

*Back cover: **Floods, Sidlaw Hills** (see also page 68).*

Contents

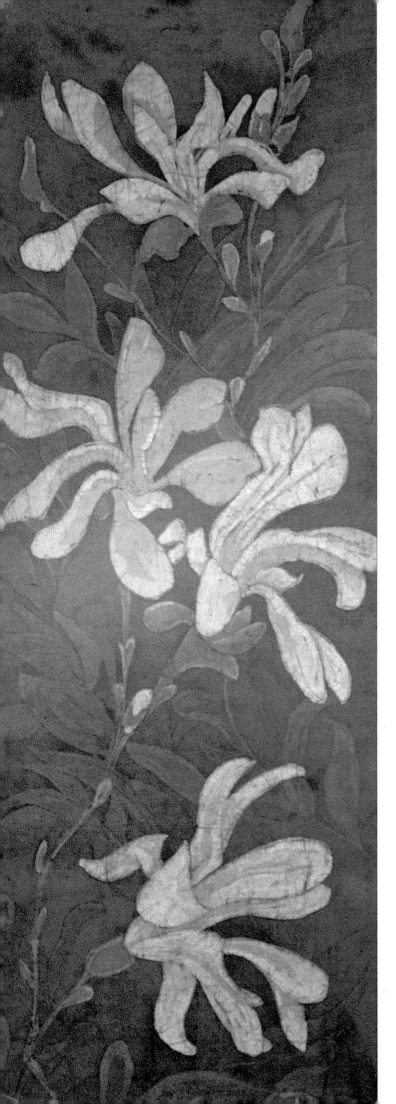

Introduction

Batik is thought to have originated, many hundreds of years ago, in India. Now, of course, it is Indonesia and Java that one thinks of as its natural home. In its oriental environment it has been used mainly for decorative purposes – to beautify clothing, especially. I have been told that the remains of royal garments have been found in ancient Egyptian tombs. The batiks that tourists bring home from visits to the Orient are mainly mass-produced, manufactured by an industrialised process. These are not the kind of batiks I am concerned with.

When carried out solely by hand, with a unique picture created of an original subject, batik can be no less 'art' than oil-painting on stretched canvas, or watercolours or chalks applied to paper.

I began doing batik after a couple of years at art school. I felt it suited me. I wanted to use dyes, in preference to oil paints or watercolours. There were marvellous colour possibilities, and it did not seem necessary to be precise and neat (as in screen-printing, for instance). That is not me, at all! Every artist needs to find that medium which exactly suits his or her personality. You must obviously get very familiar with it; you must find out how it works, and what you can achieve with it.

Like everyone else, I started my batik with simple designs and one or two colours, and I began with making patterns – really simple geometric shapes. Gradually, I tried depicting objects, like butterflies and flower heads and imaginary birds. Then – after many years! – I graduated to 'fine art', using my wax and dyes to create sophisticated, complex landscapes that could otherwise be executed in oils or watercolours.

It still comes as a surprise to many people that batik can be used for the creation of landscapes and flower studies. In this book I hope to demonstrate how, as I lead you through all the complicated but fascinating stages of producing a work of art using batik.

Magnolia Stellata.
On this batik I completed the flower heads first, and then waxed them. I drew the leaves in and added them at the end with deepening dyes.

Shadows on Evia.

This is in Greece, on the island of Evia – or 'Euboia' – and the house is owned by a friend of ours whose family has lived here for centuries. I allowed the natural cracking of the wax to suggest the look of old stone walls. One can deliberately 'crack' in certain places, to help build up certain emphases in pictures. The shadow areas are very strong, to create the 'hot' feeling of the subject.

Equipment and materials

Most of the equipment needed to produce a batik will already be available in the home or readily available from local suppliers. As you can see from my equipment, I do not believe in spending a lot of money on it.

• Old pots and kettles – for melting the wax and for boiling water for washing the batik.

• A portable cooker.

• Jugs and a large spoon for measuring and mixing dyes.

• Wax – I use plain paraffin wax. (The wax shown here is recycled wax taken from the top of a bucket after a batik has been washed in hot water.)

• Plastic screw-topped canisters for the storage of soda and salt solutions – for making up the dyebath.

• Plastic measuring spoons for the dye powders.

• Plastic or galvanised-steel buckets for washing out.

• Rubber gloves – dyeing can be a messy business and I would also recommend that you wear old clothes when working on a batik.

• Bleach – for rectifying mistakes in dyeing and for making highlights (must be used with care).

• Urea (a white odourless powder) – used to help the dye powder to mix correctly.

• Screw-topped jars for the storage of dye powders.

• A selection of brushes – some for applying the wax to the fabric and some for brushing on the dye.

• Notebook – I strongly recommend that you record all recipes used for each stage of dyeing and make reference to the quality/hue of colour obtained.

• Tape measure for sizing your fabric.

• Tjantings – I have collected a variety of these traditional oriental instruments for applying hot wax. Very good for fine line work.

• Fabric for the batik. I prefer fine white cotton, but you can batik on to silk or any other natural fibre.

• Sticks of charcoal for drawing out your design (use blackboard chalk for darker materials).

• Scissors for cutting out the fabric.

• Frame for supporting the fabric – see page 11.

8

9

Getting started

On these pages I explain the batik process for those of you who are new to this art form, and introduce you to my particular methods of making a picture.

The batik process

In batik the colours are produced using cold-water fabric dyes. However, you cannot just 'paint' dyes on to fabric – they would run everywhere, they would be impossible to control, and you would never get clear colours or recognisable shapes. So you have to use a 'resist process'. Hot, molten wax is used to resist or prevent the dye from going where it is not wanted. You cover parts of the design with wax, or draw around a particular shape in wax, and then apply dye to the enclosed area.

When designing a batik you have to plan your 'painting' in reverse (much like the negative of a photograph) because the areas that you actually paint with wax are those on which you do not want the colour to appear. You do not paint a dark background – you have to wax the foreground objects and allow the colour of the background to build up to a dark shade from the various dyes you apply!

Making a picture using the batik process is a relatively slow process; you must allow a day for each application of colour. Good depths of colour can only be achieved by allowing the dye to mature during a slow drying process. However, the rewards are well worth the effort.

There is a bonus to this seemingly complicated process: the wax can be cracked and the dye will penetrate through the cracks so that when the wax is eventually removed, fine cobwebby lines of colour are left. This gives batik its unique characteristic look. There is an art in the cracking itself; the less movement of the cloth during dyeing, the less cracking you get – some batik artists try to avoid cracking altogether.

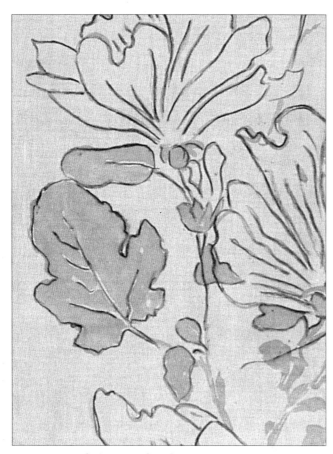

Wax must only be applied to the parts of the picture that are not going to be coloured by a particular dye.

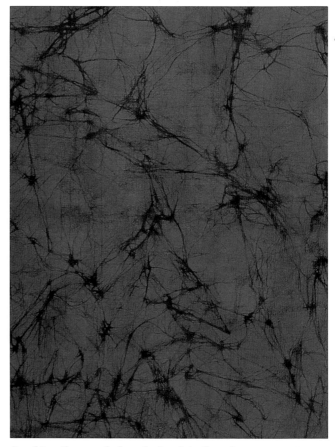

Cracking the wax before dyeing lets the colour penetrate into the cracks and create batik's unique characteristic.

Preparing the fabric

Synthetic fabrics do not hold the dye very well so you will have to use those manufactured from natural fibres. Cotton is the easiest fabric to work with, but the batik method can be used with linen, muslin, poplin, silk and satin. However, for my particular craft – painting pictures – fine white cotton is the ideal fabric. Some commercial cottons are treated with a dressing which will inhibit the effect of a dye; these cottons must be washed thoroughly before starting a project.

The fabric must be stretched and held taut so that you can work on it. Working flat on a table (with the fabric in contact with the surface) will not do because when you apply the molten wax it would penetrate through the fabric and stick to the table top, breaking the resist.

You can buy special batik frames, but you can just as well pin your piece of fabric on to an upturned box. However, I like to work on a table and I suspend the material above it using two 150 x 12mm (6 x $\frac{1}{2}$in) wooden planks. Their length is the width of my work table, and I secure them across the top and bottom of the table with four G-clamps. The planks are just thick enough to separate my work from the table when the fabric is stretched between them. The fabric is held taut by being hooked on to sharp nails which I hammered, slightly on the slant, into the planks at about 100mm (4in) intervals. (These spikes are known in the woollen industry as tenterhooks – hence the saying 'on tenterhooks!').

Alternatively, you could simply fasten the fabric on to some hooks at the top and hold the work taut with your free hand while applying the wax. This is all right for a simple design but I prefer to have both hands free.

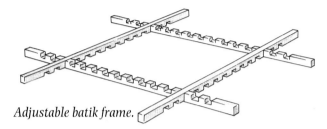

Adjustable batik frame.

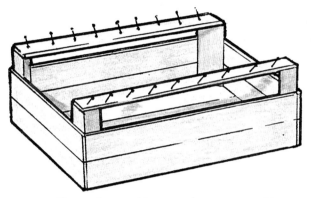

You could stretch your fabric across an upturned box.

I like to work on a table, and I fasten my fabric to nails hammered into two planks of wood which I secure to the table with G-clamps.

11

Types of wax

There are various of types of wax available: beeswax, paraffin wax and a special batik wax. Experiment with different types to find one that suits your needs. I use paraffin wax; some people say that this wax cracks too easily, and that you should use the batik wax, which is a mixture of beeswax and paraffin wax that dries harder and resists cracking. However, I like the ease of use and the versatility of paraffin wax, and I adjust my methods of controlling the degree of cracking according to the effect I want to achieve.

Selection of waxes: beeswax grains, beeswax block, paraffin wax grains, recycled paraffin wax block, special batik wax.

Melting the wax

Care must be taken when heating the wax to melt it. You can buy a special wax pot (a thermostatically controlled heater), but if you do not want to go to this expense at first, you can use a double saucepan, melting the wax over hot water. The wax at the correct temperature looks transparent when applied to your cloth. It must not be opaque, and it should form the same size shape on the reverse side of the material as on the front – you may need to peep underneath to check! This is especially important with heavier-weight fabrics.

Never leave hot wax unattended; it has a low flashpoint and will ignite of its own accord. Do not tip hot wax over yourself – the result can be very unpleasant, as I found out a few years ago! Try to isolate the heating area, and do not allow saucepan handles to project.

Mixing the dyes

Remember that dyes can colour your skin as well as a fabric, so always wear rubber gloves. Some dyes are toxic and/or poisonous, so do follow the manufacturers' safety instructions and do keep them well away from foodstuffs and children.

Cold-water dyes must be used for batik. A hot dye, of course, would melt the wax and you would lose your picture! There are many different types of cold-water dyes and various processes, too, and you will need to work out a system that you are comfortable with. The more work you do, the more you develop your own short cuts and methods.

Over the years I have tried a number of recipes for making up dyes, but the following is the one I have found best for my work. It makes 50ml (1 pint) of dye, which should be sufficient for a medium-size picture. If you are working on a large picture, or using a heavy fabric, or if you want to achieve a very strong and even colour, you will need to make up more liquid in the same proportions.

Dye powder:	a few grains up to 1½ teaspoons, according to the desired strength of colour.
Urea:	1 tablespoon.
Salt solution:	250ml (½ pint).
Warm water:	250ml (½ pint).
Soda solution:	2 tablespoons.

Salt solution

This is a saturated solution of salt in water. Fill a screw-topped container three-quarters full with water and then add salt (cooking salt, agricultural salt or water-softener salt all work well); shake the container to dissolve the salt into a solution. Continue adding salt until a deposit gathers at the bottom which will not dissolve. Only then is the solution sufficiently strong.

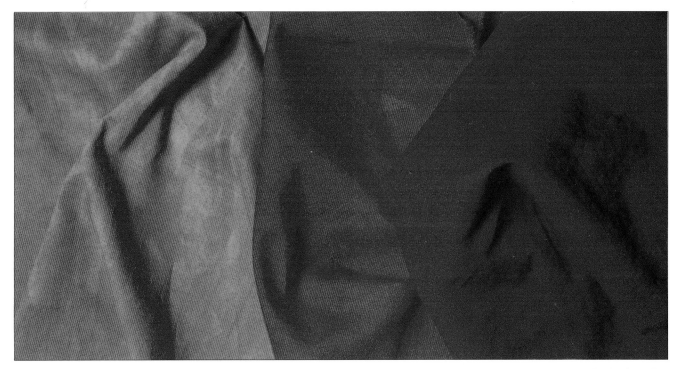

The shade is affected by the amount of dye powder in a 500ml (1 pint) dyebath. A few grains of red gives a pale pink, $^1/_4$ teaspoon a mid pink and $^3/_4$ teaspoon a dark pink.

Soda solution

This is made up in a similar way to the salt solution, except that household washing soda is added to the water until a deposit gathers at the bottom.

Urea

Urea is an odourless white powder which helps the dye powder to mix completely. It also helps the dye mature (see page 19). It can be bought at larger dispensing chemists, but is cheaper if you can track down an agricultural-chemicals supplier. A bag of urea lasts for ages!

Making up a dyebath

Mix the urea and dye powder with a tiny amount of the warm water in a jug or small plastic container, until all is well mixed and dissolved. Then add the salt solution, the remainder of the water, and the soda solution. The dye is now ready for use. You can either transfer it to a dyebath or, if you are going to brush it on to the fabric, use it direct from the container.

Use a strong plastic spoon for mixing dye, and plastic measuring spoons for adding the dry ingredients. Keep accurate records of each batch of dye. Finally, do not forget to wear rubber gloves!

Use plastic measuring spoons to add the dry ingredients to the dyebath recipe, and always wear rubber gloves.

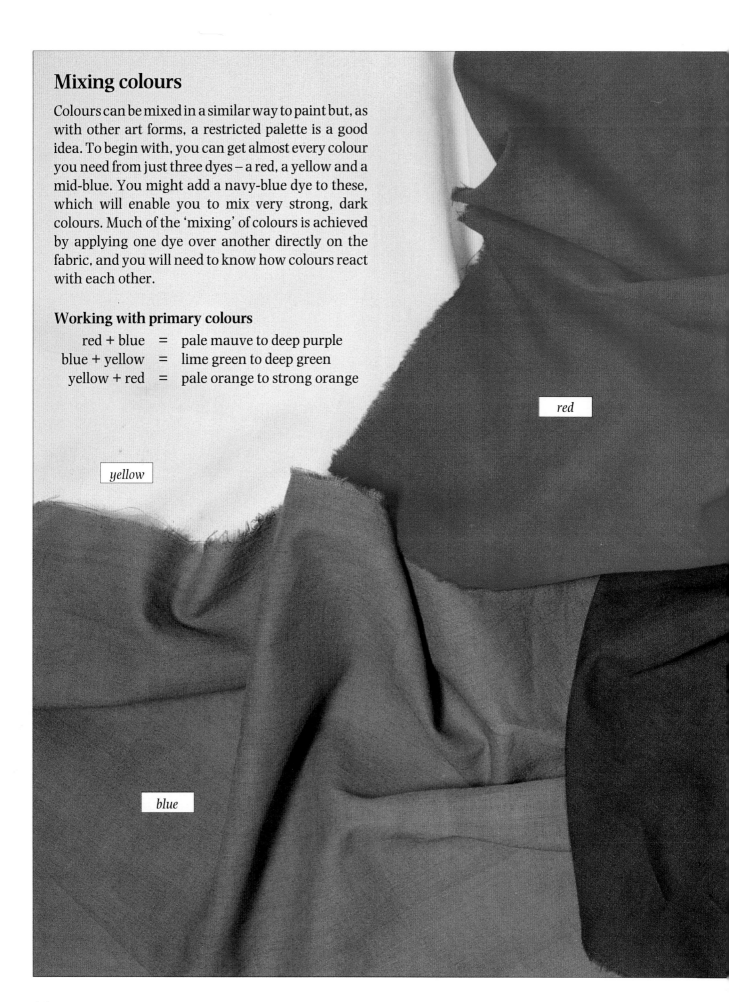

Mixing colours

Colours can be mixed in a similar way to paint but, as with other art forms, a restricted palette is a good idea. To begin with, you can get almost every colour you need from just three dyes – a red, a yellow and a mid-blue. You might add a navy-blue dye to these, which will enable you to mix very strong, dark colours. Much of the 'mixing' of colours is achieved by applying one dye over another directly on the fabric, and you will need to know how colours react with each other.

Working with primary colours

red + blue	=	pale mauve to deep purple
blue + yellow	=	lime green to deep green
yellow + red	=	pale orange to strong orange

red

yellow

blue

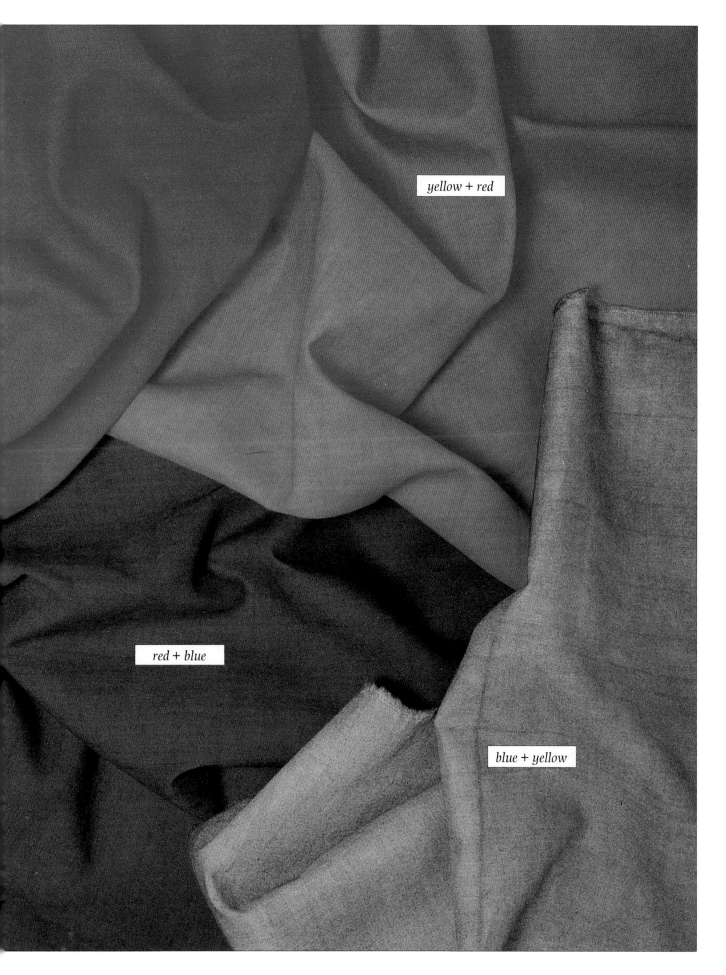

yellow + red

red + blue

blue + yellow

Mixing primary and secondary colours

$$
\begin{aligned}
\text{red} + \text{green} &= \text{brown} \\
\text{blue} + \text{orange} &= \text{brown} \\
\text{yellow} + \text{mauve} &= \text{brown} \\
\text{red} + \text{yellow} + \text{navy} &= \text{black}
\end{aligned}
$$

Building up colour

As a general rule of thumb it is always better to begin dyeing a batik with pale shades of colour, deepening the shade and colours by overdyeing with the same strength dye or with stronger colours.

It is almost impossible to change strong dark colours once you have applied them – you can do a certain amount of alteration by applying bleach instead of dye but I shall say more about this later (see pages 55 and 63).

Scarlet, blue and yellow dyes (¹/₄ teaspoon of each) produced this brown colour.

Shades of the same colour can be produced by overdyeing with successive dips of the same-strength dyebath. First I dyed the whole piece. I then waxed the top one-third of the fabric and dyed again. Finally I waxed the top two-thirds and dyed again.

Use charcoal to draw your initial design and to reinstate it as the work progresses. Here I am referring to my original sketch, painted in oils, to add further details prior to waxing.

Drawing the design

To get a picture started I draw the initial shapes on to the fabric using sticks of charcoal – charcoal shows up better than pencil and washes off easily (on dark material you could use blackboard chalk). I find it useful to make a rough sketch of the design on a piece of paper so that I have a reference from which I can reinstate any lines that disappear during successive applications of dyes, or when the fabric has to be washed out to remove the wax. In the early stages this loss could make you lose track of which side of the cloth is the front side.

To help you identify the front side I suggest that when you start a batik you should wax your signature, or some other mark, on your work so you know which side you are looking at. I always use the bottom right-hand corner as I look at the picture.

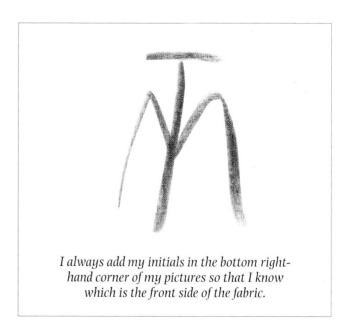

I always add my initials in the bottom right-hand corner of my pictures so that I know which is the front side of the fabric.

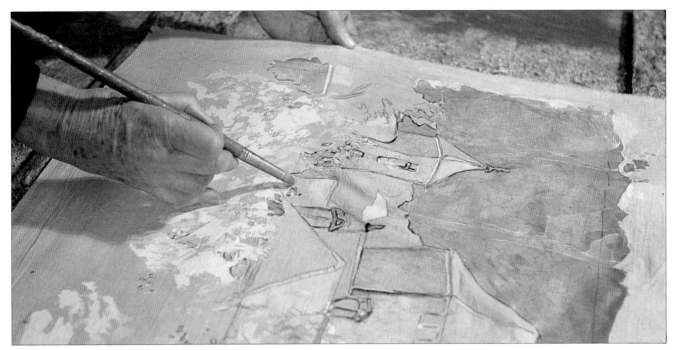

I like to use a variety of different-sized brushes to apply the wax.

Applying the wax

To apply the wax you have a choice: you can brush it on, especially when you want to cover large areas; or you can use the traditional oriental instruments called 'tjantings'.

I like to use brushes: I find that the fairly tough bristle oil-painting brushes are best and I have a variety of sizes. You can use house-decorating brushes – the bigger sizes are very useful when you want to wax a large area quickly.

Tjantings are little copper 'pipes' with tiny spouts, from which the hot wax flows. Working with tjantings is similar to using a pen – you can literally write and draw with them. There are many designs of tjanting, offering a range of spout sizes to govern

Traditional tjantings can be used to in a similar way to a pen to add fine lines of wax.

the width of the waxed line. They can be difficult to control, but when you have mastered them, without dripping wax in all the wrong places, they are good for fine lines and for graphic work.

Dyeing colours

For all-over applications of dye colour, immerse the fabric in the dyebath and leave for between five and ten minutes. If you want the full strength of the dye, do not hurry with this stage. Remember that if the fabric is scrunched up in the dyebath some cracking will occur. If you do not want a cracked effect then you can apply the dye with a brush on stretched fabric, or you can lay the piece of fabric on a few layers of old newspaper and sponge it on. Do look on the underside of the fabric to make sure that the colour has penetrated right through.

Maturing and drying

After dyeing the fabric, roll it up in newspaper and lay it aside to mature for up to twenty-four hours. The slower the dye matures, the better is the end result. To avoid getting frustrated while waiting to get on with the next stage, I try to have between four and eight pictures in production at any one time. A good system is to work on four pictures one day and another four the following day. In this way, one lot are drying while you work on the others. Sometimes – particularly in the early stages – two batiks could have the same dye applied; this speeds things up.

Washing out

During the production of the batik, and definitely at its completion, you will have to 'wash out' the fabric – in other words, get rid of all the wax. Do not worry, the colour is fixed and it will not boil away!

Place the batik in a clean bucket and pour boiling water over it. When the water has cooled, skim the cold, hard wax off the surface to reuse. Repeat the washing process again to ensure that all the wax has been removed.

If you can find an old wash-boiler that *really* boils it will be ideal for washing out your batiks, especially if you have to remove wax from large objects such as bedspreads or wall-hangings. Whatever you do, never pour hot waxy water down a drain; it will block up very quickly and could be disastrous!

If you want to eliminate cracking in the waxed parts of the picture apply the dye with a sponge.

Roll the dyed fabric in newspaper and allow to mature for up to twenty-four hours.

I am fortunate enough to have an old sink that I use for dyeing and washing out my fabric.

Experimenting with dye colours

When you have learned the basics of the batik process, I would suggest that you experiment on some scrap pieces of fabric before attempting to get down to some serious work. Here are two exercises for you to try. Use different dye colours and keep notes about the recipe used, the time the fabric is in the dyebath, the maturing time and your impressions of the resultant colours.

Four colours overdyed without washing out

In this exercise you will be making a picture of different-coloured concentric circles. The sequence shows what happens when you dye a series of colours without washing out the wax between each dye colour. The idea is to try and have a white centre (of course, there is no white dye; by white I mean the natural colour of the fabric). However, this is more difficult than you may think, especially if you do not rewax any previously waxed areas.

For this exercise I have used four dyes – yellow, red, deep red and navy blue – but you can use whatever colours you choose.

1. Prepare a square of white fabric and draw a circle with a piece of charcoal. Fill the circle with wax, immerse the fabric in the yellow dyebath, then take it out and allow the fabric to dry.
2. Now draw in another circle on the yellow background, larger than the first one. Apply a band of wax around, but not over, the original circle, immerse the fabric in the red dye and then let it dry.
3. Wax a further ring on the resultant orange, then dye with a deeper red and dry the fabric.
4. Finally wax yet another ring on the deeper red, and dye deep blue to give a purple colour on the background.

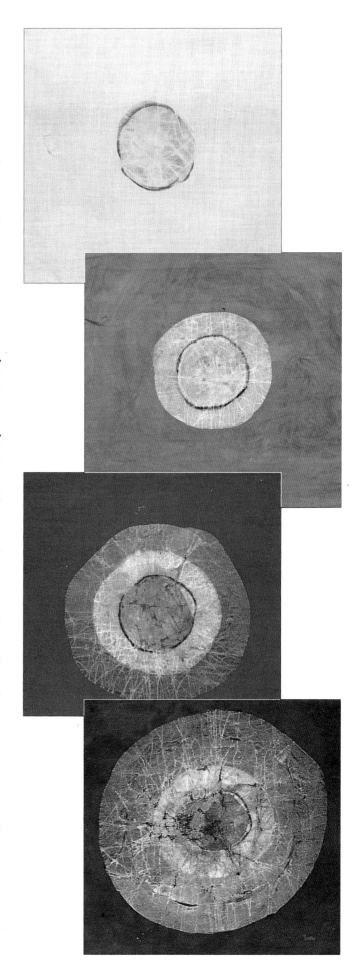

20

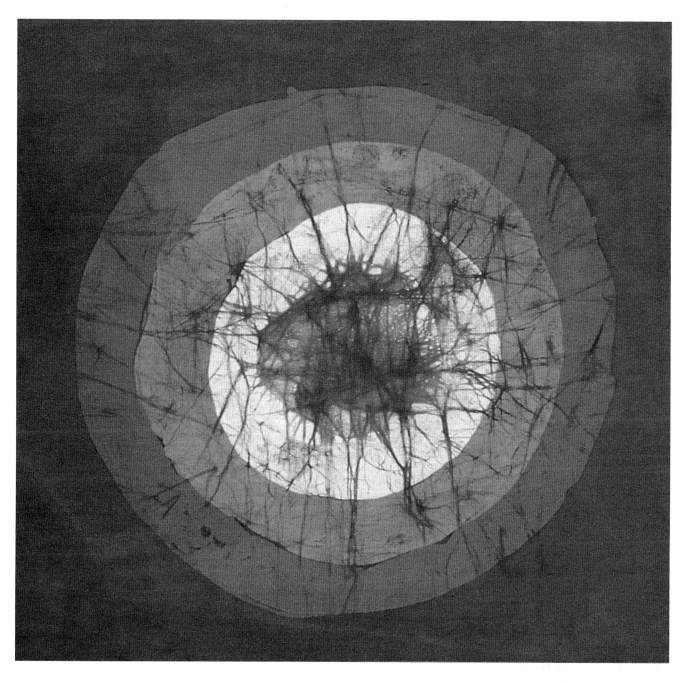

5. Wash, dry and iron the fabric to show the finished result. Note how the 'white' centre has almost disappeared under all the cracking.

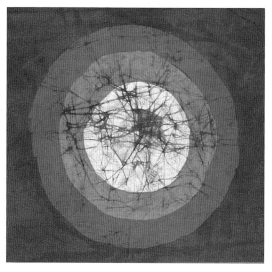

This is another piece of fabric that went through the same process as above using exactly the same dyes. The random cracking was uncontrolled, showing just how impossible it is to do two batiks exactly alike. They may be similar in colour but the cracks will always be individual!

Two colours overdyed after washing out

In this exercise the wax is washed out after each dye has been applied to the fabric. If you are careful when you immerse the fabric in the dyebath you should eliminate any cracking.

1. Draw a diagonal line across a square of fabric, carefully apply wax to one half, making sure that you do not crack the wax, and then dye with a red.

2. Wash out the wax with boiling water and allow to dry. You now have a square with one white triangle and one red triangle. Now draw another diagonal line in the other direction and apply wax to one side (i.e. across one half of each of the white and red triangles).

3. Carefully immerse the fabric in green dye.

4. Wash out the wax and allow the fabric to dry. The result is four different-coloured triangles from two dyes. The triangle that was waxed prior to the application of both dyes remains white; red over white gives red; green over white gives green; green over red gives a sort of brown (in this example the red was pinkish, and the green bluish – hence, not a true brown!)

Stage 1.

Stage 3.

Stage 2.

Stage 4.

Using colours for pictures

Getting to grips with the effects of one colour over another is of particular importance when you work on flowers and landscapes. You will need to know exactly what successive dyes will do to those that have gone before. For this reason I cannot stress enough the need to experiment, and to keep notes.

Right: This is a detail from the batik picture of dahlias that appears on the front cover of this book. I first dyed a strong red-orange, followed by a pale scarlet, a deep crimson red and a purple for the shadows on the petals. All of these colours helped to create the dark background which also had a deep navy added as the final colour.

*Below: **Castlerigg.** These standing stones were initially drawn as a sketch. This subsequent batik measures 120 x 90cm (48 x 36in). The light parts of the stones and area of the sky were waxed first and the colours of the background were also used to make the shadows on the rocks.*

Making a flower batik

Mallow flowers

It is time to start on something more demanding – a batik of flowers, perhaps. The first thing to do, quite obviously, is make up your mind what flowers you feel you would like to make the subject of a batik. Here I have chosen a pink mallow.

1. If the weather and circumstances are right, it is nice to draw the initial sketches *in situ*, but you could equally well cut some sprays and bring them into your studio. In any case, draw the flowers from various angles so as to understand them thoroughly. Search out their special *characteristics* – neat or sprawling, angular or round. Pay particular attention to the way the leaves join the stems . . . the way the veins run . . . where the shadows lie, or darkness of colour.

A good idea is to number the different flower heads on your sketch, so you can check which one you are working from later on. It is also a help, where leaves and petals are near to each other and muddled, to identify them by adding a letter G, for green, if it is a leaf, and a P for pink, if it is a petal. This will be a guide when deciding the different dye areas. You could do coloured sketches, of course.

Stage 1.

24

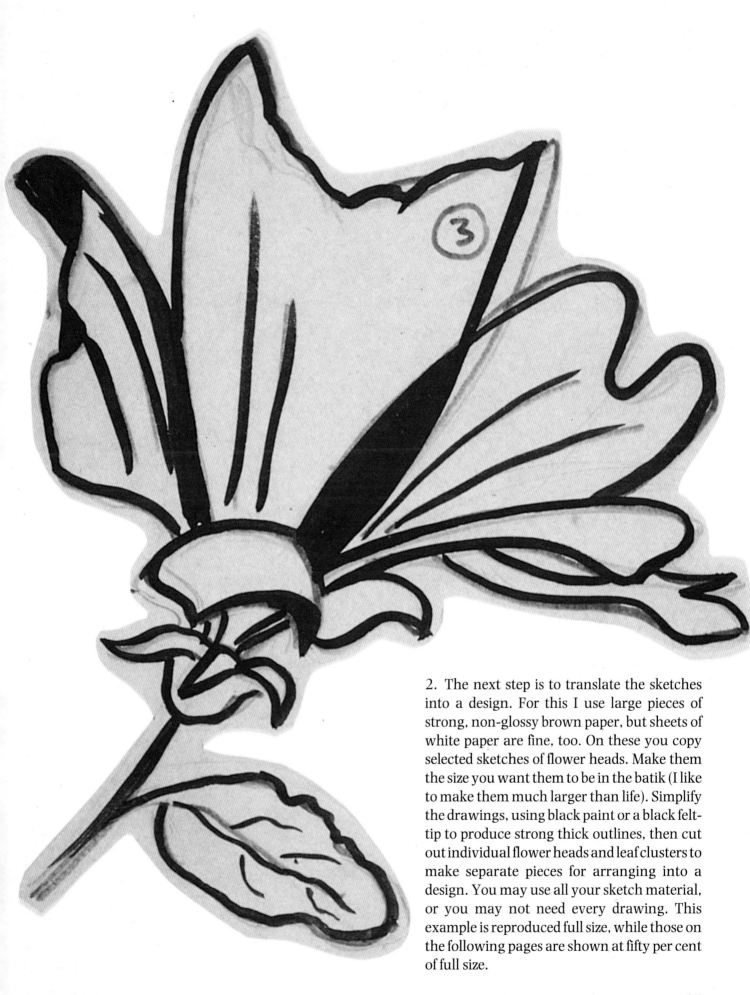

2. The next step is to translate the sketches into a design. For this I use large pieces of strong, non-glossy brown paper, but sheets of white paper are fine, too. On these you copy selected sketches of flower heads. Make them the size you want them to be in the batik (I like to make them much larger than life). Simplify the drawings, using black paint or a black felt-tip to produce strong thick outlines, then cut out individual flower heads and leaf clusters to make separate pieces for arranging into a design. You may use all your sketch material, or you may not need every drawing. This example is reproduced full size, while those on the following pages are shown at fifty per cent of full size.

Stage 2.

3. Lay out your fabric and position the main pieces on top, juggling them about until you find a pleasing composition. For this batik I cut some fabric approximately 120 x 45cm (48 x 18in), but you can work any size you like. Perhaps, to start with, you would feel happier with a smaller, more traditionally sized picture about a third of this size, maybe with just one flower head on it.

Stage 4.

4. If the fabric is fine enough, you may be able to lay it on top of the paper shapes and to draw the design on to the material using charcoal. Otherwise you must devise another method of transferring it – you could use the shapes as templates and draw round them, or you could apply charcoal to the reverse side of the paper shapes and press the image down on to the material. I draw in the linking stalks and leaves when the flower heads are in position.

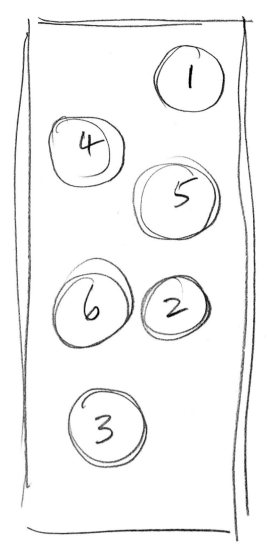

Stage 5.

Stage 6.

5. Do a very rough diagram on another bit of paper as a reminder of where each shape is to go. You will find this helps as a reference.

6. Decide on the colours you are going to use. For this picture I am using shades of mauve and pink for the flower petals, green for the leaves and stems, and dark blue for the background. These colours are all made from red, blue and yellow, the depth of colour being governed by the dilution ratio of water to dye powder. Stretch your fabric, heat up the wax, and start.

Wax in the stalks and leaves and outline the flower petals and veins as thinly as possible with a very fine brush. If you drop wax anywhere it is not wanted, boil some water and carefully rub with a little brush until the wax has been removed.

The charcoal drawing will start to disappear during successive dyeings and it is easy to become muddled. For flower batiks you will find it really helpful to draw in the outlines of the whole design with wax before you start to dye. You can always dye dark over the lines after washing out. Fine outlines of wax will almost certainly 'break' during successive dyeings, so you may want to rewax them every now and then.

29

7. When the wax is cold, dye a pale pink-mauve, then roll up the fabric in newspaper to mature and dry.

8. When the first dye is dry, start waxing the lightest parts of the petals. Here it helps to refer to your original sketches which show shadows and veins, etc. The important point is always to remember to leave the parts that are to be darkest unwaxed, for future dyes to deepen them. Now dye again, using the same strength of colour. Over the first dyeing, it will make the shade deeper. It is difficult to see this because the waxed area looks darker than the surrounding un-waxed part, but if you hold the batik up against the light you can see a paler shade under the wax.

9. Wax more of the petals and then dye a third time using almost the same colour again, but with a little more of the red and less of the blue, to make the veins and shadows a slightly stronger red colour.

10. Now wax over the entire flower petals, going over earlier cracks. You do not want cracks of the next colour, a deep blue, to appear in the flowers. Turn the fabric over and wax the reverse side; there may be places where the wax has not totally penetrated.

Dye the fabric with navy blue – you might prefer deep blue – using a sponge. At this stage I do not want to increase the cracking, which would happen if the fabric was moved about in a dyebath, so I do not immerse the batik but sponge the dye on, with the picture flat on newspaper as shown below.

Stage 10.

Apply the dye with a sponge to avoid cracking the wax.

Stage 11.

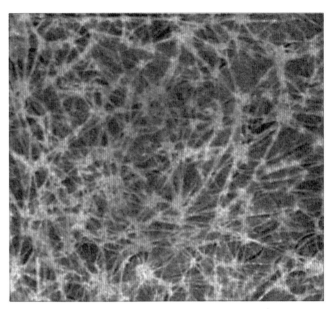

Stage 12.

12. Now stretch the picture again, wax the entire background and crack it very thoroughly.

Stage 13.

11. When the deep blue is dry, wash out, dry and iron the batik. The white outlines of the flowers and the white veins can be clearly seen.

13. Start waxing the flower petals, leaving the white lines and any areas that you want to go a deeper colour unwaxed. You might prefer to wax the white lines too; as in all art it is a personal decision – at each stage you have to re-assess the picture and decide what the subsequent stages will do to it.

Brush the green dye on. It will not matter too much if you do run over, as you will be going to dye pink, then red, and any green in the wrong place will go brown-red, which will help the shadows. Turn the picture over, and repeat the dye on the reverse side.

Stage 14.

14. Continue waxing the green leaves and stalks and then dye with a pale-pink dye, similar to the one you used at the very beginning. This will get rid of any white outlines.

Stage 15.

15. Wax the edges of the petals and any part of the flower that you do not want to go a deeper shade and then dye a colour similar to the third dye – red with a little blue.

16. Finally, when the fabric is dry again, wax the remaining areas of flower petals, and dye with a strong scarlet. This should go into the cracks of the background and also add a subtle emphasis to the edges of flowers and to the leaves. (This is just my idea to give the batik a bit of excitement – a colour slightly different from all the rest!)

Stage 16.

17. When this last dye is dry, wash out the batik, iron it and, if you like it – frame it!

The finished batik.

Gallery of flowers

Here are some of my favourite flower batiks. Large simple shapes and strong colours can be used in batik in a very decorative way.

Each batik has its own problems, which need to be sorted out before you begin, and to help you I have given some notes about each picture.

◁ *Dog Roses.*

I dyed the rose petals with three pale dyes of pink, then waxed them and dyed the centres strong yellow. Finally I waxed all over the flowers so that the background could go deep blue.

▷ *Omani Flowers.*

The background of this study was never waxed, so all the dyes used added up to make it dark.

Romneya.

In this picture I waxed the flowers carefully right at the start, leaving the shadow areas of the petals to go very pale grey. As with all the flower studies, following the lines of a very detailed drawing is a great help.

Cistus.
Here I added to the leaves of the background each time a dye went on, so I ended up with a jumble of leaves, deepening in colour, to contrast with the white flower heads.

◁ **Yellow Lilies.**
Sometimes a small area of strong colour is best isolated and done either at the beginning or at the end of a batik. In this picture the red stamens were put in right at the end. They were surrounded by wax and dyed a strong red. At times like these, a thickener, such as Manutex, can be added to the dye to stop it from spreading.

Amaryllis. ▷
Here I wanted to add more interest, so I put in evening primroses to provide contrasting colour. Extra leaves were added as the work proceeded.

*◁ **Passion Flowers.***

The background in this case is white, so it was waxed right at the start of the picture and left throughout all the subsequent dyeings.

Hypericum. *▷*

This is where a tjanting came in useful to make the fine hair-like lines when waxing the stamens. It would have been more difficult to do this with a brush.

Creating landscapes

Landscapes are, perhaps, the most difficult of all subjects to bring off successfully in a batik. But it can be done, and the results are often more striking than if more traditional media had been used.

With its complex, subtle colours, a landscape will probably be waxed, dyed and washed out many times during the making of a picture, and I make no apology for reminding you of the help it will be to make a list of colours to be used, and in what order. It is particularly important in a landscape to work out the colour scheme in advance, because reds and greens will probably be used and, as I think is clear from the exercises in the early part of this book, these colours need careful control if one is to retain their purity. The order of use is perhaps even more important – often you need, when you start, to wax not only the white areas (clouds, for example), but also the other areas where the initial run of colours you intend to use must not go. When you have gone as far as possible with one colour sequence, you will have to stop and wash out, dry your picture, iron it, redraw it (the charcoal lines will disappear during the dyeing process), decide what colours you want to keep and start waxing these to begin a new colour run. On a large batik you may need to stop and wash out perhaps four times during the course of creating the picture. If you dye five or six times, say, without washing out, the wax cracks too much and breaks down; the colour floods into the cracks and you are likely to get a nasty dark mess!

In this chapter I show you, stage by stage, how to create two landscape pictures. The first, a village scene in France, is a conventional landscape depicting the local colour and architecture. The second is much freer in its composition and is my interpretation of the misty hills outside Hollywood in America.

The Crannoch, Ardanaiseig.
This batik has large expanses of 'white' water and sky where the cracking plays an important part in creating texture. The dark railings and trees are made up of all the dark dyes used in the picture.

45

My original oil sketch.

St Martin de Vers, Lot, France

This is a very pretty part of France, and I often take painting holidays in the area. I painted the oil sketch below on one such visit. It was a lovely bright morning with clear light and strong shadows. The ancient church, with its massive rectangular tower, pierced by pigeon holes, soars out of the surrounding roofs. It is a beautiful subject for a painting, but the sketch is only the beginning of what will be a long and involved journey – translating the picture into a batik that captures the essence of that scene. On the following pages I take you through all the stages.

The finished picture will be about 60 x 43cm (24 x 17in) in size, but I shall work on a slightly larger piece of material. Fabric does not behave like paper: it can stretch and shrink slightly. An extra border will also give me freedom to alter the composition slightly when I come to prepare the batik for exhibition and will also provide for turning the edges over a backing when framing.

Stage 1.

1. Trace the basic structure of the picture on to the cloth with charcoal.

2. Begin the batik process by waxing the 'sunlit' sides of the buildings and chimneys, some of the highlights of the bushes, and the other areas that you want to end up green. It is a matter of dealing with the lightest parts of the picture first – the deep colours will come through lots of subsequent dyeings.

Mix yellow, red and blue dyes in tiny amounts to give a pleasing warm beige, and immerse the batik in the dyebath. Using very weak solutions of dyes often gives a patchy result – the colour is taken up rapidly by the first part of the fabric that is immersed – but remember that many more colours are going to be added to the picture.

Stage 2.

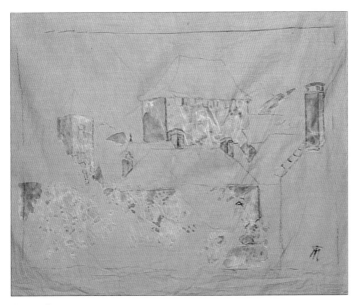

3. When the first dye is dry, wax the 'shadow' side of the buildings and chimneys and the light part of the fields, then apply a very pale blue dye to begin work on the sky.

4. Wax the cloud areas and the wall of the building in the right foreground, just suggesting the broken surface of stones. Rewax any cracks in the initial waxing to try and keep light areas light. Dye pale blue again.

Stage 3.

Stage 4.

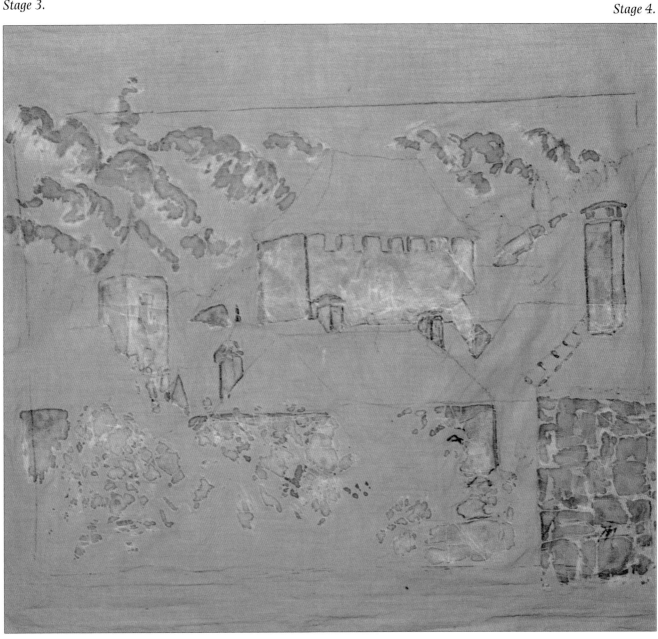

Stage 5.

5. When that, too, is dry, wax some more of the leaves on the bushes and the part of the sky that is to be lighter blue – the upper right part of the sky will take the next dye, and go a deeper blue. Now wax the lightest side of the red roofs, and rewax the cracks again in areas that you want to keep pale. Dye a deeper blue.

6. Next day, wash out for the first time, then dry and iron the fabric.

Stage 6.

Stage 7.

Stage 8.

7. Redraw any details that have disappeared during the previous stages and then wax all areas that are to remain blue: the sky, of course, and the deep shadow areas. You must also wax the pale walls and any other colour you want to keep! Then dye lime green.

8. Now wax any of the green areas that you want to keep and put on a blue dye everywhere else; this makes the shadows go a little deeper. The blue also helps to build up the very deep shadows of the foreground trees and shadows under the roofs. You must not go too deep with this dye, however, as you will be using reds and oranges next time over the blue to get the right colour for the roofs.

9. Wax all green areas apart from the underside of the leaves, and the deep shadows, and then dye orange (red and yellow dye mixed).

10. Next, wax the lightest sides of the red roofs (and any cracks you do not want any more colour to run into!). Dye with a mixture of red and yellow and a few grains of blue. This will darken the existing dye and give a deeper colour for some of the roofs.

Stage 9.

Stage 10.

11. Wax more of the roofs and dye pale blue.

Stage 11.

Stage 12.

Stage 13.

12. Wax the remainder of all the roofs, leaving dark shadows (under eaves and windows, etc.) clear, and concentrate on the foreground bushes. Dye dark blue mixed with yellow to give a greenish tinge to the brown colours in the foreground.

13. Now wax the dark tree-trunks and the distant eaves and windows and then use the same dye to make a really deep green elsewhere. This will be the final dye, and will make the deep brown area go blackish.

14. Now wash out and iron the finished batik. Draw in the outline of the picture with charcoal to indicate the edges for framing.

Stage 14.

Here is the completed work.

Original oil sketch.

Hollywood Hills

Now we will now try a rather freer subject, which calls for further processes.

I have been fortunate in having been able to travel quite widely in my quest for good subjects for landscapes. A year or two ago I accompanied my husband on a business trip to Los Angeles. Early one evening, when visiting friends who lived in the western suburbs, I looked out of the panoramic window of their high-rise condominium and saw a magnificent sunset over the Hollywood Hills. My American hosts watched, intrigued, as I scribbled the view on the back of an envelope, carefully adding colour notes.

When I came back home, I used these scribbles to paint the oil sketch above, which then became the reference for this batik project.

Stage 1.

1. Draw the rough outlines of the hills on a piece of fabric sized to allow for a turn-in border .

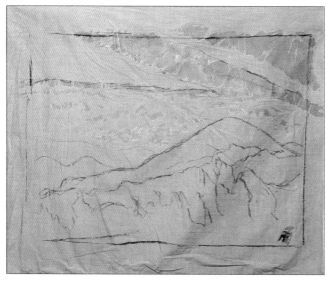

Stage 2.

trees will be darker and also lit by the evening light, they can be left unwaxed to take this pale apricot hue. They will become progressively darker with the subsequent dyes.

3. When the pale apricot colour has dried, wax the clouds immediately below the limit of the first area of wax and dye pale apricot again.

When preparing this project I realised that I had made a mistake! I did not wax all the pale blue sky area in the beginning, and the apricot dye ended up in areas where it ought not to be. Luckily, the batik had not gone too far and I was able to retrieve the situation by removing the apricot colour in the offending area with bleach. This part of the picture will be dyed pale blue later to get the right shade. I sponged the bleach on with the batik flat, so that the chemical did not run into the wrong places! I then rinsed the whole picture with cold water, and rolled it up to dry before continuing.

2. Start by waxing the white cloud tops and the areas of sky that are to be pale blue. You are going to dye apricot colours first, and as the mountains and

Stage 3.

55

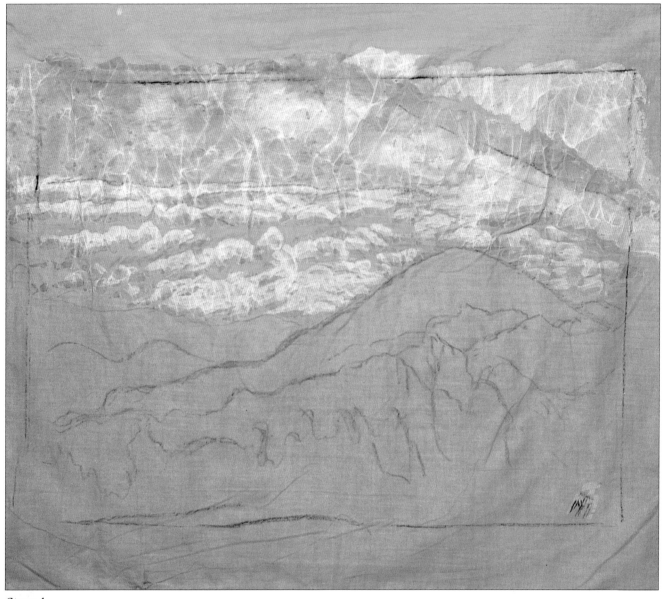

Stage 4.

Stage 5.

4. Continue waxing more of the clouds below the limits of the earlier waxing to create the impression of clouds that are lighter on the top than on the underside. (I have also waxed the areas of blue sky that I missed earlier.) Now dye apricot colour again.

5. Next, wash out, dry, iron and then redraw the picture (the drawing is not always necessary).

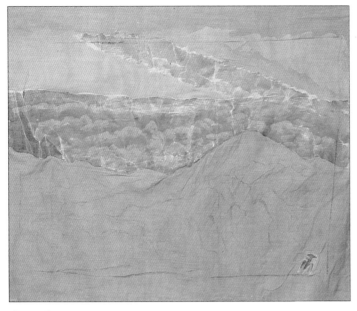

6. Wax the apricot part of the sky and the white cloud areas, leaving just the blue areas and the mountains and trees unwaxed. Dye with the next colour, which is pale blue.

Stage 6.

7. At this stage draw in the hills and wax the most distant one – and of course, the pale-blue sky! Dye pale blue again.

Stage 7.

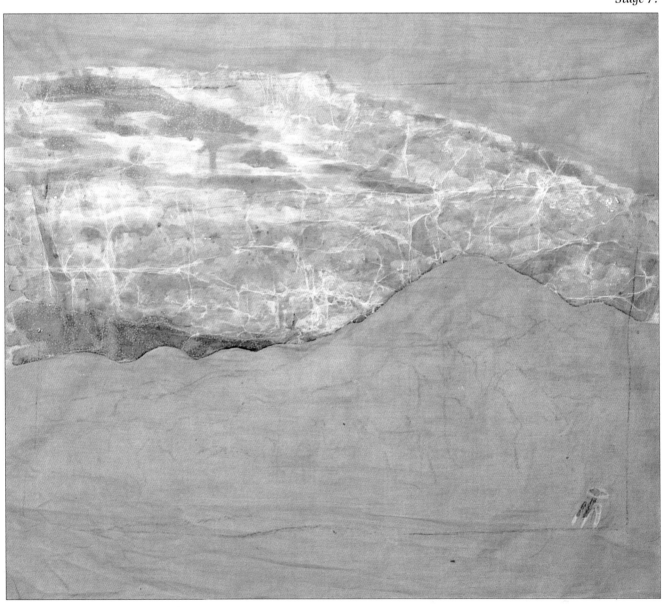

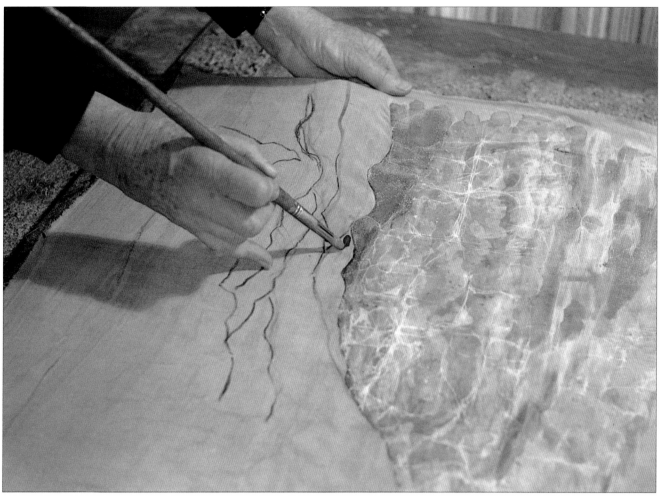

Stage 8.

8. Continue with the work of waxing to suggest 'layers' of hills, and also wax the lower part of the hills, where it is misty.

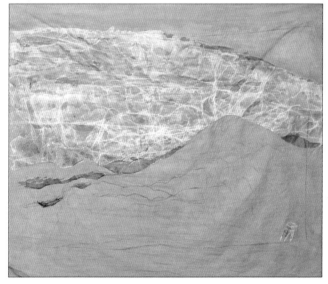

Stage 9.

9. Dye apricot, to get a little more light and colour in the picture.

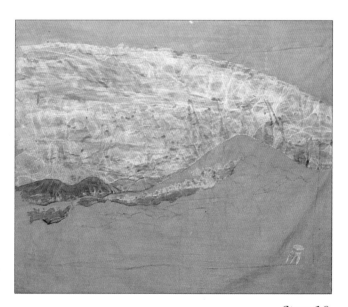

Stage 10.

10. Now repeat the routine: carry on waxing the nearer hills, and rewax the cracks above the principal hill, to keep a clean line. However, this time dye with a blue colour.

Stage 11.

11. Again, repeat the actions of the last stage and then dye with apricot.

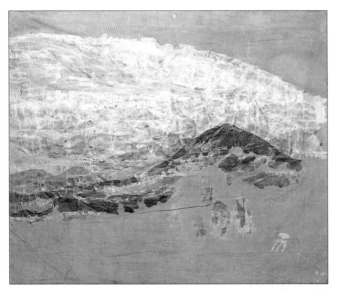

Stage 12.

12. Next, redraw the foreground trees and bushes and wax the remainder of the hills behind them. Start to wax the centres of the bushes (the edges of them should be silhouetted). Dye this stage blue again.

Stage 13.

13. Again, wax outwards from the centres of the trees and then wax a little of the edge of the upper band of cloud. Dye medium green/blue.

Stage 14.

14. The wax on the light part of the sky area is now getting 'tired' and tending to flake. You do not want deep colours to run into it, so play safe and sponge the next dye (a green/blue) on with the batik flat on the work-table, instead of immersing it. This retains the dye in the foreground area.

Stage 15.

15. When the fabric is dry, continue to wax towards the outside edges of trees, leaving the outer shapes to go darker once more. Dye deep green/blue again.

Stage 16.

16. You want to allow the tops of the trees on the left to go even deeper in tone – where the 'sunlight' is likely to make the contrast greater – so wax the remainder of the trees and the bushes on the right. This will help to make the foreground a little more varied. Once more, dye deep green/blue.

Stage 17.

17. In this next stage you now going to introduce a different process – using bleach to remove colour, instead of dye to build it up. The intention is to give the impression of sun, just glinting over the tops of the hills with rays of light. To do this, crack the wax over the distant hills (the batik is already quite cracked but you want it more pronounced in this place). Wax any unwaxed areas of trees and rewax the principal hill, as you do not want it to have bleached cracks.

Sponge on the bleach over the cracked areas, rinse, and then dye apricot – this will fill the bleached cracks with colour. The dark cloud at top right was left unwaxed and the apricot dye makes it greyer.

Stage 18.

18. When the material is dry, wash out and iron the finished batik. Indicate the edges of the picture with charcoal ready for framing .

The finished picture.

Gallery of landscapes

Everybody has his or her own approach to creating a work of art. Obviously, different things inspire different people. To me, all subjects need to have a characteristic quality of their own: perhaps a strange colour scheme; an odd sky formation; unusual shapes of buildings; a sad feeling or a light, sunny one. . . All these emotions help to establish the kind of picture that will (or should!) emerge from your labours.

The following pictures are reproductions of some of my landscapes. I have added some notes to describe how to overcome some of the particular problems I encountered when making them.

Weston Longville.

In this view from our house in Norfolk, the sky was the picture – that is what made me want to do the scene in the first place! I began by waxing the 'cloud' area three times and dyeing the sky with pale creams and pinks (no other drawing had been done, so these dyes went over the whole fabric). I washed out and waxed part of the colours I had already dyed and then dyed another three cream/pink colours. Again I washed out, and finally put three more dyes on the sky – to make a total of nine colours. I then waxed the whole sky and proceeded with the foreground.

Suffolk Field.

Again it was the sky that intrigued me. The batik went along more or less straightforwardly until it was all but finished. But I then had to use bleach to create the rays of light. I use dilute household bleach for this, but it is a very tricky procedure. I had to draw the rays in and wax all the other areas, then sponge the bleach over the rays (taking care to keep the batik flat to prevent running). I kept stopping during the process to put the picture under a cold running tap before applying the bleach again. You must never leave the chemical to work on its own, otherwise you may return to find the rays completely white and the picture underneath totally disappeared! I finished by sponging over vinegar and water to neutralise the bleach and stop it from having any further effect on the picture.

Roofs, Viana do Castelo.

It is surprising where one gets inspiration. This was the view from my hotel window in northern Portugal. The very detailed sketch for this picture needed several days to do. The sketch is a kind of shorthand for me, not a picture in its own right. In this batik, the terracotta-coloured roofs needed many dyes, waxing one or two roofs at a time, then dyeing the remainder until the deepest-colour roof was waxed.

65

In Alpes Maritimes.

Saint Agnes is up in the mountains behind Monaco. To get a two-colour sky – the apricot colour at the bottom and pale ice-blue at the top – I waxed the complete sky and cracked the lower half only, very thoroughly. Then I dyed apricot and washed out the fabric. This gave apricot 'cracks', just in the lower half. I rewaxed the sky and only cracked the upper half, then dyed it ice-blue. It was washed out again, and the sky completely waxed, before I continued with the remainder of the picture, which of course had a mixture of apricot and ice-blue dyes over it, giving a dull green as a basis for waxing some of the trees. The walls, etc., were waxed right at the start of the picture and rewaxed after the first washing out.

Cotignac, Evening.

This is a relatively undiscovered part of France, in Var. It suggested a very peaceful still picture. It was evening, and again I concentrated on the sky, particularly on the cloud, which was what made me want to do the picture in the first place. The white part of the clouds was waxed first, then pale orange was dyed below and pale blue above in a single stage. This saved time, but of course it meant that the dye had to be sponged on, with the material flat and not immersed in a dyebath. The grey part of the clouds was built up later, after the remainder of the sky had been completely waxed.

Floods, Sidlaw Hills.

My husband's ancestors lived in this part of Perthshire, above the River Tay. It was flooded when I saw it. This subject, again, needed very careful drawing. As in the picture Towards Dunwich (page 70), the waxing of the background was important in building up the dark branches and reflections.

Flatford.

Flatford is steeped in art – the associations with John Constable are everywhere. In this picture the leaves and branches had to be waxed and dyed in stages, gradually making each shade slightly deeper as more colour was added. Finally the background had to be completely waxed to allow yet more dyes to go on, to make the foreground reflections darker.

Towards Dunwich.

I often walk my lurcher dog over this wild stretch of country near the Suffolk village that disappeared under the sea centuries ago. It was one of the most difficult batiks I have done, because the dark brambles had to be constantly drawn in, and only the background colours waxed, so all the various dyes built up to make the twigs and brambles appear dark. As I have already said, you cannot 'paint' dark shapes; you can only outline the background with wax.

Misty Hills.

It is difficult to do mist and snow scenes in batik. All you can do is gradually deepen the dyes. If you strengthen the colours too quickly you get hard edges of colour which 'jump' out in the wrong places. I referred earlier to the fact that you have no white as in painting, so you have nothing to make colours opaque!

Craig More.

In this study of a mountain near Aberfoyle in West Perthshire, the mixture of scarlet, mid-blue and warm yellow gave a cheerful impression. Only three dye colours were used on this batik and that shown opposite.

Trossachs Evening.

In this evening picture, the tones are more sombre. Deep blue, bluish red and lemon dyes were mixed and used throughout.

Cruel Sea.

I love doing these sea studies. This batik had many dyes, with subtle changes of colour, yellow being the final one, to create the feeling of churned-up sand in the immediate foreground. Cracking was used to give texture and colour, the yellow dye seeping through the cracks in the wax in the foreground.

Santa Cruz Island.

There is no white at all in this picture. The sea off the California coast at Santa Barbara was this strange shade of lavender-pink for about ten minutes every evening. Initially the batik was dyed overall pale pink before any waxing was done. (It could, of course, have been done on pale-pink pre-dyed cotton!)

Scottish Storm

This is one of my early batiks. I sketched it as an oil, actually kneeling in a Scottish field in the rain, surrounded by sheep! I could not resist such a dramatic subject, with its lovely strong colours! This is what attracts me to spend my time making landscapes in batik.

Olives, Evia.

This composition needed careful thought – the yellow areas had to be waxed first and I started dyeing with the blues. The batik was washed out and I then started on the yellows and greens. The soft tones of the olive foliage was difficult to achieve – it took a long time to find the exact mix of dyes.

Reed beds, Walberswick.

*This is a large batik, measuring 120 x 90cm (48 x 36in), with a very dramatic
sky. The rich brown of the reeds is a deeper tone of the sky.*

Exhibiting your work

Batiks are, perhaps, most often seen displayed as wall-hangings, often attached to bamboos or lengths of wooden dowelling; reflecting the oriental origin of the technique, no doubt. These purely decorative batiks, which are those most often encountered, undoubtedly look attractive that way. Sometimes they are 'mounted' on a backing of contrasting fabric, which gives added support for larger batiks or those done on heavier materials. They are also occasionally edged.

My batiks, however – landscapes and flower studies done as fine art – suggest, I believe, a more formal treatment. They are no less 'pictures' than oil paintings or watercolours, and need to be displayed as such – unframed and stretched over thick chipboard, or, as I prefer, sympathetically framed.

Of course, the fabric is not as robust as canvas, and will benefit from additional support before it is put into a frame. To my mind, cotton or silk looks rather flimsy and vulnerable when mounted on a stretcher like an oil painting. Probably the best thing to do is back it with hardboard, tucking the edges round and attaching them to the reverse side with adhesive tape or fabric adhesive. I always paint the hardboard support white beforehand, because I find this gives an added luminosity to the picture and helps keep the colours true. (With thin fabric, the colours look a bit dead over unpainted hardboard).

Personally, I prefer not to cover batiks with glass. They are not, after all, fragile and subject to becoming grubby, like watercolour paper. If they do get dirty they can easily be cleaned – more so than oil-paintings!

Probably few other media are quite so easy to handle – you can unframe them, wash and iron them, or, if you wish, put them into new frames to suit an altered décor. Nothing as drastic is likely to be necessary, though. Early batiks of mine look the same now as they did when I completed them, more than twenty years ago! I have no doubt that they will endure every bit as long as the oils, watercolours and pastels other artists are creating.

Pink Poppies.
The waxing of the flowers here was carefully contrived to capture the 'crinkly' character of the petals. The background was bleached before dyeing sky blue; blue over pink would give a mauve, and I did not want a mauve background.

Index

Procopi, Evia. The red roofs were all waxed to start with and the blue-greys of the landscape dealt with first.